LOST LINES OF WALES
THE MID WALES LINE

TOM FERRIS

GRAFFEG

CONTENTS

Moat Lane
Llanidloes
Pantydwr
St Harmons
Rhayader
Newbridge-on-Wye
Builth Wells
Erwood
Talgarth
Brecon

FOREWORD

For many of us who love railways and are absorbed by their history, there is always that sense of regret for those lines that got away. These are routes which were closed long before we were ever able to travel on them and which are known to us only from what remains of their formations and structures today, in photographs or the flickering 35mm amateur films made by railway enthusiasts in the 1950s and 60s.

I suspect that the subject of this book, the line that ran through mid Wales from Moat Lane Junction near Caersws to Brecon, is high on that list of those which many of us would love to have experienced for ourselves in its heyday. All that is left of the line today are parts of its track bed and some of the stations for which other uses have since been found.

Following the route the line took by road, one is struck by the enduring beauty of the landscapes though which it passed and also perhaps by the relatively few houses, farms and villages along the way. Like all railways, the Mid Wales Line sought as level a path as could be found for its tracks. In this instance that was achieved by following river valleys. It began by running through the Upper Severn Valley as far as Llanidloes. From there its trains ran beside the River Dulas, finding a gap in the hills at Tylwch to pass into the valley of the River Marteg. Afterwards it would reach Rhayader, from where it followed the River Wye for much of the rest of the way to Brecon. The views from the windows of one of the three or four trains which ran daily along its full 60 mile length must have been unbelievably picturesque in spring, summer and autumn, if rather more daunting in winter.

This was a classic rural railway and once its virtual monopoly on the limited amount of both passenger and goods traffic generated by the districts it served was challenged by the inexorable rise of the internal combustion engine in the years after the Great War, it is not surprising that its fate was sealed in the early 1960s, with closure coming just short of the 100th anniversary of its opening.

INTRODUCTION

Railways came relatively late to mid Wales. In the 1830s several schemes were mooted but not pursued to build lines through the area largely composed of the old counties of Brecnock, Radnorshire and Montgomery, mostly in connection with reaching ports on the west coast to capture a share of the traffic to Ireland. The Railway Mania of the 1840s saw lines promoted that would in time run through the Welsh Marches to connect Newport, Hereford, Shrewsbury and Chester, but there seemed little traffic potential to attract investors to lines to the west of this axis. This began to change in the early 1850s with the result that in the space of about 15 years a whole network of routes had been promoted and built through the counties mentioned above. This was put together in a piecemeal and unplanned fashion by a number of small companies, but it did deliver the benefits of railway communication to these hitherto remote and largely agricultural districts. While many lines have closed, a truncated version of this network still survives into the new millennium.

The initial part of what was to become the Mid Wales Line which ran from Moat Lane Junction to Brecon, was built by the Llanidloes & Newtown Railway, the first in the area authorised by Parliament, receiving its Act in 1853. It was initially isolated from any other railways, but was soon joined by a number of other small independent companies which eventually completed lines linking Aberystwyth to Whitchurch and Shrewsbury. The L&N took six years to complete its 13 mile route but was rescued from isolation in June 1861 when the Oswestry & Newtown Railway opened. By way of a branch from the Shrewsbury to Chester line from Gobowen to Oswestry dating from 1848, Llanidloes, Newtown and Welshpool were now linked to the national railway network. Initially most trains from Oswestry ran through to Llanidloes.

Meanwhile, another independent company had been incorporated to extend the railway west from Newtown. This was the Newtown & Machynlleth.

Authorised by Parliament in July 1857, it opened in January 1863. The N&M branched off the L&N line in a north westerly direction just before Caersws at a spot initially called Caersws Junction, though for most of its existence it would be known as Moat Lane Junction. This left Llanidloes as a terminus for a time, though it would shortly become an important station on a new through line to Brecon when the Mid Wales Railway was promoted.

The interaction between railway companies in the nineteenth century as they competed for territory and revenues is often complicated and the Mid Wales Line is no exception to this. Two routes were being promoted in the late 1850s to serve the middle of Wales. One was the line that still exists, the Central Wales line running from Craven Arms, on the Shrewsbury to Hereford line, through to Carmarthen and Swansea. It was built in the 1860s by three separate companies backed by the powerful London & North Western Railway. Meanwhile, another scheme, the Mid Wales

Railway, was promoted to build an extension of the existing L&N route from Llanidloes south to Newbridge-on-Wye and then on to Llandovery along with another line south through the Wye Valley towards Brecon. Parliament approved the latter but not the line to Llandovery.

At this point matters were complicated by the intervention of the Manchester & Milford (See the volume in this series, Lost Lines of Wales, Aberystwyth to Carmarthen) a company destined never to get near either of the locations in its title and one of the least successful of all the Welsh railway companies. The M&M received an Act in 1860 to build a line from Llanidloes to Pencader in Carmarthenshire. From those two places existing railways would be used to take its traffic to other destinations north and south. From Llanidloes traffic would pass over the lines being built to Oswestry and Whitchurch in the general direction of Manchester and south of Pencader the Carmarthen & Cardigan Railway would carry it to Carmarthen and towards Milford Haven.

The M&M line was to run to Llangurig and then over bleak, high, mountainous terrain to Devil's Bridge where it would divide, with a branch going to Aberystwyth roughly along the route taken to this day by the narrow gauge Vale of Rheidol Railway with the other line heading for Pencader. By 1861 construction had started on the Mid Wales Line and the eastern part of the M&M. Both companies would share tracks the first 1½ miles south from Llanidloes, the M&M line diverging at a point known as Penpontbren Junction. Construction of the M&M route stopped when it reached Llangurig as doubts arose as to the wisdom of forging through the mountains to Devil's Bridge. It is believed that one goods train ran through to Llangurig before the line was abandoned without seeing any regular traffic. Several attempts were made to revive this route and others connecting the Mid Wales Line to Aberystwyth in the 1860s, but nothing ever came of them. The tracks from Penpontbren Junction to Llangurig were removed in the 1880s making this one of Wales' shortest lived and least successful stretches of railway. With the failure of its plans to reach the Mid Wales Line, the M&M eventually had to content itself with a line linking Carmarthen to Aberystwyth.

With the M&M debacle behind it, construction of the Mid Wales Line to Brecon continued. At the southern end of its route the Mid Wales had other issues with which to contend. The Brecon & Merthyr Tydfil Junction Railway was launched in 1858 and its trains started running from Brecon to Pant near Dowlais in April 1863 (See Lost Lines of Wales, Brecon to Newport). Leaving Brecon B&M trains used the trackbed of a tramway opened as long ago as 1816, which connected the canal at Brecon to Hay-on-Wye and Eardisley. This was the intended route to the town of yet another railway which was converging on it, the Hereford, Hay & Brecon, authorised in 1859. In the end ownership of the tramway was apportioned to the Mid Wales and the B&M. The latter got the section from Brecon to Talyllynn Junction and the Mid Wales that from Talyllynn north to Three Cocks Junction.

This took its name from a nearby inn and was the point where the lines from Llanidloes and Hereford converged at the village of Aberllynfi, near Hay. Both the HH&B and Mid Wales Lines opened in 1864, sharing the track between Three Cocks Junction and Brecon.

The initial service was of three passenger trains and two mixed trains conveying goods and passengers. These were operated by the contractors who had built the line, Watson and Overend, and ran from Brecon as far as Llanidloes. In 1864 the companies which had built the line from Machynlleth to Whitchurch amalgamated to form the Cambrian Railways and were joined in 1865 by the Aberystwyth & Welch [sic] Coast Railway, which had opened its line from Aberystwyth to Dovey Junction and was extending it along the shores of Cardigan Bay to Pwllheli. The Mid Wales was not part of this new company and passengers changed to CR trains at Llanidloes to complete onwards journeys through Moat Lane Junction to destinations in other parts of Wales or England. The other line serving the area, the Central Wales Extension Railway, opened to Builth Road in November 1866, crossing the Mid Wales Line at a higher level. A connection was built between the two lines, allowing goods traffic to be exchanged between them.

The Mid Wales began to operate its own trains from 1866 when the contractors failed. It acquired locomotives, carriages and wagons, setting up a works to maintain them at Builth Wells, probably one of Britain's less well known and certainly one of its shortest lived railway workshops. The line did not prosper and the hoped for flows of coal traffic from south Wales did not materialise, except briefly during the Great War when the so-called Jellico Specials, conveying Welsh coal for the Grand Fleet to its Scottish bases, used the line.

It remained a rural backwater, though one significant boost to its traffic came in the 1890s, when Birmingham Corporation began work on dams and aqueducts in the Elan Valley west of Rhayader. This brought clean water, fed by gravity, to provide for the needs of that rapidly expanding city over 70 miles to the east. A railway system, at its greatest extent it had some 33 miles of standard gauge track, was constructed to supply materials to the construction sites.

The Cambrian Railway, which had been working the Mid Wales Line since 1888, acquired the line in 1904, making this the last major addition to its already extensive network of lines in the centre of Wales. One early consequence of this was the closure of the Mid Wales' erstwhile Builth Wells workshops in 1904, its functions being transferred to the CR works at Oswestry. As a CR line, at the grouping of Britain's railways in 1923, the route from Moat Lane Junction to Brecon became part of an enlarged Great Western Railway. With the creation of the publicly owned British Railways in 1948, the line came under BR's Western Region.

The pattern of services on the line remained remarkably consistent throughout the near 100 years of its existence. The earliest extant timetables from the 1860s show three through trains from Llanidloes to Brecon and one on Sunday. These took around two and a half hours for the 52 mile journey. With the CR now working trains through to Moat Lane Junction, in 1903 there were three trains over that slightly longer distance, taking between 2 hours 35 minutes and 2 hours 45. The solitary Sunday train seems to have disappeared from the timetables by the 1940s. In the last year of its existence in 1947, the GWR was offering three through trains, all taking around 2 hours 45 minutes, and a British Railways timetable from 1961, the year before closure, was not dissimilar to that in terms of frequency, or lack of it, and the time taken for the journey. In addition to the trains which ran from Moat Lane Junction through to Brecon, there were usually short workings at both ends of the line timed for scholars.

Many will associate the destruction of a large part of our railway network in the 1960s with Dr. Richard Beeching, who became Chairman of the British Railways Board in 1961. His notorious report, The Reshaping of British Railways, published in 1963, called for the closure of one-third of the country's 7,000 railway stations, the withdrawal of passenger services from around 5,000 route miles of track and the shedding of 70,000 British Railways jobs. However, the fate of the Mid Wales Line and indeed all the railways which served Brecon had been sealed before Beeching started to wield his axe.

There had been no attempt to modernise the line in the 1950s with the introduction of diesel railcars, which were tried on many minor lines by BR to improve service times and frequency. It remained steam worked to the end, with engines being provided by the sheds at Moat Lane Junction, Builth Wells and Brecon. Whilst it continued to be a delight for railway enthusiasts and provided a service for isolated communities, it is hard to see how it could have survived much longer given the sparse traffic and limited services it carried. The closure notices were posted in 1962 and efforts were made to provide replacement bus services to diminish the hardship that the loss of the railway would cause. Some freight traffic, mostly trains of cement used in the construction of another dam in the Elan Valley, lingered on between Moat Lane Junction and Llanidloes until 1967, but the last public passenger trains ran on the Mid Wales Line on 31st December 1962, consigning the line to the pages of railway history.

BRECON

For the second time in this series our journey begins at Free Street station in Brecon, but instead of heading south to tackle the Seven Mile Bank on the way to Newport (Lost Lines of Wales, Brecon to Newport) we are going north this time on a 60-mile run along the Mid Wales Line. This will take us through the old counties of Brecknock and Radnorshire to Moat Lane Junction between Newtown and Caersws, on the line from Aberystwyth to Oswestry and Shrewsbury. On 29th March 1948, the 5.05pm departure from Brecon is headed by ex-GWR Dean Goods 0-6-0 No 2543, one of a long lived class of locomotives which were regular performers on this route for many decades. Though the publicly owned British Railways took over the running of the country's railways from 1st January 1948, No 2543 still flies the flag for her former owners with the initials GWR just about discernable through the grime on the side of her tender. The carriages of the train are also still in GWR livery.

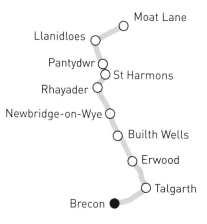

Moat Lane
Llanidloes
Pantydwr
St Harmons
Rhayader
Newbridge-on-Wye
Builth Wells
Erwood
Talgarth
Brecon

Trains to Newport and the Mid Wales Line shared the first four miles out from Brecon to Talylynn Junction, where the routes divided. This part of the line dated back to 1816, when it was built by the Hay Tramway. The tunnel which brought the track into Talylynn Junction has a strong claim to being the oldest railway tunnel in the world. Pausing at the Junction with a Mid Wales service is LMS designed 2-6-0 No 46503, one of a class of 128 locomotives that entered service between 1946 and 1953 and were regular performers on this route. No 45603 was built by BR at Swindon in 1953 and withdrawn in 1967.

TALGARTH

From Talylynn Junction the line headed off in a north easterly direction, passing through the remote Llangorse Halt. Opened by the GWR in 1923 in the hope of attracting visitors to the nearby Llangorse Lake, the largest natural lake in Wales. It then travelled through a station somewhat distant from the village of Trefeinon before reaching Talgarth, where the station was sited conveniently close to the centre of this agreeable small town. 2-6-0 No 46523, one of the last batch of these engines built at Swindon in 1953, pauses with a train from Brecon to Moat Lane Junction on a pleasant summer's day in the late 1950s.

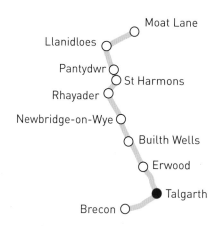

- Moat Lane
- Llanidloes
- Pantydwr
- St Harmons
- Rhayader
- Newbridge-on-Wye
- Builth Wells
- Erwood
- Talgarth
- Brecon

2-6-0 No 46508 pauses at Three Cocks Junction on a Mid Wales Line service bound for Brecon.

About 2 miles beyond Talgarth, the line came to Three Cocks Junction, where the Mid Wales Line diverged from that to Hay and Hereford. The station took its name from a fifteenth century coaching inn which is still extant, rather than the nearby village of Aberllynfi, which in turn took its name from the place where the River Llynfi meets the Wye. This was another of those many locations in Wales that was created by the arrival of the railways, and like many remote country stations and junctions it was marked by long periods of somnolence followed by brief ones of hectic activity when trains arrived on the scene. The station had four platforms, two on each line. In this view, a train from the Hereford line is on the right of the picture while two Mid Wales services cross at their platforms to the left. Both locomotives are Ivatt designed 2-6-0s, the one on the Brecon train, to the left of the picture, is No 46525.

The Mid Wales Line headed on a north westerly bearing from Three Cocks Junction, closely following the River Wye. After a distance of about three miles it came to the station of Boughrood & Llyswen, which served villages on either bank of the river. They were also in two different counties, Llyswen in Breconshire and Boughrood, which was nearer to the station, in Radnorshire. The locomotive in this undated view of a train bound for Brecon is another of the ubiquitous Ivatt 2-6-0s. Happily, this engine, No 46512, is one of seven members of the class to have been preserved. Today she is to be found a long way from Mid Wales, being based at the Strathspey Railway in Scotland.

Above: No 46512 pauses at Erwood with a train for Brecon, showing the staggered platforms at the station to good effect.

Between Boughwood & Llyswen and the next station, Erwood, about four miles further on, the GWR opened a very basic halt with a short wooden platform to serve the hamlet of Llanstephan in 1933. Erwood was and indeed still is an attractive station with staggered platforms, meaning they were not opposite each other. On 28th August 1959, services hauled by two of the LMS designed 2-6-0s cross at the station. On the left, unusually running tender first, is No 46514 on a short working from Three Cocks Junction to Builth Road, whilst sister locomotive No 46504 is in charge of a Moat Lane Junction to Brecon train. Erwood station, in a pleasant location close to the River Wye and easily accessible from the nearby A470, has been beautifully conserved and is in use as a tea room and an art gallery. A diesel shunting locomotive, carriages and other railway artifacts add to its ambience.

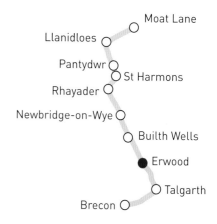

With the line still heading in a north-westerly direction through the Wye Valley, five miles beyond Erwood it came to Aberedw a station which opened in 1869. This was located on a curve well above on the river. At one time it had possessed a signal box and it retained sidings for goods traffic until closure, though it is hard to believe that the small village it served would have generated much of that. Facilities were fairly basic: a name board, waiting shelter and a seat; the lamp post on the platform does not seem to have any means of illumination. The low platform here and at other locations along the line meant that portable steps, seen here in front of the waiting shelter, had to be provided to assist passengers descending from carriages.

BUILTH WELLS

Builth Wells was the first sizeable town the Mid Wales Line served since leaving Brecon though to put this in context, Builth and the neighbouring location of Llanelwedd, home of the Royal Welsh Show, have a population of about 3,000 today and it would have been less than this when the railway was in its heyday. Builth was the location of the workshops of the Mid Wales Railway which closed after the Cambrian Railways took over the line in 1904, but it remained a busy station with extensive goods facilities. On 15th September 1949 a northbound goods train crosses a passenger train for Brecon at the station. The locomotive No 893, the former CR No 99, was one of only eleven ex-Cambrian standard gauge engines, all 0-6-0s, which survived to enter BR stock in 1948. No 893, built by Beyer Peacock in 1908, was extensively modified by the GWR during their period of ownership and withdrawn by BR in February 1953.

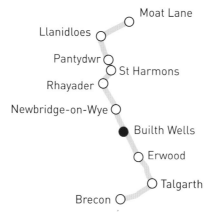

- Moat Lane
- Llanidloes
- Pantydwr
- St Harmons
- Rhayader
- Newbridge-on-Wye
- Builth Wells
- Erwood
- Talgarth
- Brecon

Builth Road, a couple of miles north west of Builth Wells was a fascinating place, where the Mid Wales Line crossed the Central Wales Line, which ran from Craven Arms, on the Shrewsbury to Hereford route, to Swansea. From 1869, this line had been owned by the London & North Western Railway and after grouping in 1923 it passed to the London Midland & Scottish Railway, remaining a place where a wide variety of locomotives could be seen. The location of the two lines in relation to each other is well illustrated in this view taken on 15th September 1949. At the Low Level Mid Wales station is the 1.10pm passenger service from Brecon to Moat Lane Junction, in the hands of ex-GWR Dean Goods 0-6-0 No 2556. The Swansea bound passenger train at the High Level station is hauled by ex-LMS Black Five 4-6-0 No 45298. The coaches forming the Shrewsbury bound train at the other high level platform are also of LMS origin.

Some Mid Wales Line services started and terminated at Builth Road. On 30th May 1936, GWR 0-4-2T No 4874 is ready to depart for Brecon on such a working. This locomotive was the last of a class of 75 introduced in 1932. They were fitted for Auto Train working which meant that they could propel specially fitted Auto Trailers, coaches which had a driving cab at the end. This meant that the loco did not have to run round its train at termini, a facility particularly useful when working branch lines. When the train reached the end of the line, the driver moved to a driving cab in the front of the first carriage where he had controls linked mechanically to the engine to drive the train. The fireman stayed with the locomotive to attend to the fire and water. On this occasion, the two elderly coaches with clerestory roofs in the GWR chocolate and cream livery which make up the train were not fitted for this type of operation, so No 4874 will have had to run round them before heading back to Brecon. A Central Wales line service is seen at the High Level station, the white tower of wooden construction was a luggage lift connecting the two stations.

There was also a physical connection
between the two routes at Builth Road
which was by means of a line which
opened in 1867 and ran from north of
the Mid Wales Line station up to the
Central Wales line south of its station.
This connection is in the foreground
of the picture, which also shows a
former LNWR 0-8-0 with a short goods
train on the high level line on 15th
September 1949.

The classic view of the Mid Wales Line at Builth Road is that taken looking down on it from the High Level station or the path leading to it. The locomotive at the head of this goods train bound for Moat Lane Junction is Dean Goods 0-6-0 No 2516, the sole survivor of the 260 engines of this type built by the GWR between 1883 and 1889. No 2516 is on display appropriately in Swindon at the Museum of the Great Western Railway there.

NEWBRIDGE-ON-WYE

Four miles beyond Builth Road was the small town of Newbridge-on-Wye. On 15th September 1949, the 2.40pm train from Moat Lane Junction to Brecon approaches the station, hauled by another Cambrian survivor 0-6-0 No 896 dating from 1908. The three GWR carriages, probably weighing about 100 tons, would not have taxed the loco too much even on this hilly line.

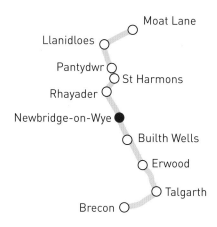

Moat Lane
Llanidloes
Pantydwr
St Harmons
Rhayader
Newbridge-on-Wye
Builth Wells
Erwood
Talgarth
Brecon

The Mid Wales Line had stayed close to the River Wye since leaving Three Cocks Junction, though it had only needed to cross the river once thus far, south of Boughrood & Llyswen station. Another crossing was required just north of Newbridge-on-Wye where the river looped to the west and this high girder bridge was required to take the line over the river.

Doldowlod station was four miles north of Newbridge-on-Wye, close to the village of Llanwrthwl, however it took its name from a country house some miles distant, Doldowlod Hall, which was the country seat in the early 1800s of James Watt, the Scottish born engineer who is seen as one of the pioneers of the development of the steam engine in the eighteenth century. Just out of the picture to the right is a siding and a loading bay, which was sometimes used to stable a banking locomotive if one was required to assist a heavy northbound train up the steeply graded section of track from here to Rhayader. In this undated view, LMS designed 2-6-0 No 46522 arrives at the station with a train from Brecon.

Opened just south of Rhayader around 1896 was Elan Valley Junction, where the extensive network of railways constructed in connection with the building of Birmingham Corporation's dams in the valley joined the Mid Wales Line. At its peak, the railway system in the Elan Valley had over 30 miles of track, on which ran steam locomotives owned by the Corporation. The double junction to the dams, seen here branching off to the right of the photograph, was reduced to a single line connection by 1908 as construction work began to wind down, dating this view to before then.

Rhayader station is in the distance as a southbound service leaves the town and heads towards the short 268 yards long Rhayader tunnel. The locomotive is one we have encountered before, the now preserved BR built Ivatt-designed 2-6-0 No 46512.

RHAYADER

The Driver is looking back for a green flag from the Guard before setting off from Rhayader to run on towards Moat Lane Junction. What may be the solitary passenger who has left the train here is heading out of the station on a path that might today be seen as perilously close to the running line.

Beyond Rhayader the line reached Marteg Halt, opened by the GWR in 1931, no doubt to attract ramblers to this remote and beautiful part of Wales. This was situated close to where the River Marteg enters the Wye and at this point the railway finally parted company with the Wye which it had followed for so long. Passing through Marteg Tunnel, the north east end of which can be seem behind the train hauled by an unidentified Ivatt designed 2-6-0. It crossed the River Marteg and then followed the valley of this river through a most picturesque mountain landscape.

ST HARMONS

The railway followed the River Marteg for most of the way to the next station, St Harmons, which was about three miles on from Marteg Halt. St Harmons had just the one platform and thus trains could not cross here. The small signal box controlled the level crossing and access to a siding behind the photographer. The blades of the points leading to this can just be seen in the foreground. One of the ubiquitous 2-6-0s, No 46515, pauses at the station on a service to Moat Lane Junction. The station and the hamlet it served took their names from a nearby church which had been an ecclesiastical site since the early Christian era. The rector of this church for a time in the 1870s was that famous diarist of rural life, Francis Kilvert. Some Ordinance Survey maps identify the church as St Garmons. The name in the railway timetables may be a corruption or an anglicisation of this.

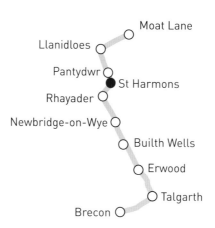

Moat Lane
Llanidloes
Pantydwr
St Harmons
Rhayader
Newbridge-on-Wye
Builth Wells
Erwood
Talgarth
Brecon

PANTYDWR

Pantydwr station was the highest point on the whole 60-mile long line between Brecon and Moat Lane Junction. The summit there, at 947 feet above sea level, was also by some way the highest on the whole Cambrian system, 254 feet higher than the more famous Talerddig summit on the CR main line between Caersws and Machynlleth. (See Lost Lines of Wales, Shrewsbury to Aberystwyth.) Pantydwr was approached by stiff climbs from either direction, of which the seven miles of almost unbroken gradients from Llanidloes was the more daunting for engine crews. Pantydwr possessed a signal box, passing loop and goods sidings. In October 1955, a pair of 2-6-0s Nos 46508 and 46522 are crossing at the station.

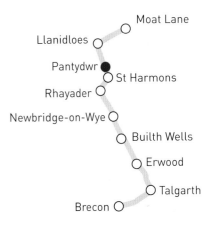

Moat Lane
Llanidloes
Pantydwr
St Harmons
Rhayader
Newbridge-on-Wye
Builth Wells
Erwood
Talgarth
Brecon

The line now followed another river valley, that of the Dulas, to reach Tylwch. This had originally been classified as a station, but in 1953 it was downgraded to the status of a halt. The signal box was closed, the remains of the plinth on which it sat are to the left of the pole and the passing loop, which served the platform to the left of the picture, becoming rapidly overgrown, was also removed at this time.

Between Llanidloes and Tylwch, the railway crossed the Dulas four times. This bridge over the river was located about half a mile south of the site of the short lived Penpontbren Junction, where the ill-fated Manchester & Milford Railway's line to Llangurig joined the Mid Wales route. The track to Llangurig remained in situ between 1864 and 1883, when it was lifted, surely one of the shortest lived sections of railway in the whole of Wales and certainly the least used. In this view, taken on 14th July 1962, the train heading towards Llanidloes is hauled by 2-6-0 No 46507. This is coasting down the grade but trains in the other direction faced a stiff climb from Llanidloes to Pantydwr.

LLANIDLOES

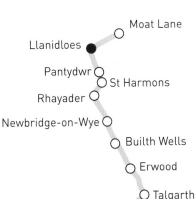

Moat Lane
Llanidloes
Pantydwr
St Harmons
Rhayader
Newbridge-on-Wye
Builth Wells
Erwood
Talgarth
Brecon

After a journey of 52 miles from Brecon, the Mid Wales Line reached the large and splendid station of Llanidloes. On the face of it this was ludicrously grand for a small town in Mid Wales, but it must be remembered that it was built as the headquarters of the very first line to open in the whole area, the Llanidloes & Newtown Railway, so I suppose its directors were entitled to indulge themselves. When the L&N amalgamated with the other companies in the area, Llandiloes was left with this legacy from its original owners. The Mid Wales Railway ended at Llandiloes and at first passengers had to change trains here to progress to Moat Lane Junction and further afield. Matters improved when the Cambrian worked the line from 1888 onwards, finally absorbing the smaller company in 1904. In this view, taken on 14th July 1961, the small extension on the left of the building housed the Gentlemen's toilets, and in the centre part of the main building by the bay window was the Booking Office and Waiting Room.

Llandiloes possessed an engine
shed and the timetables usually
included a few short workings to
Moat Lane Junction or beyond, on
which Llandiloes based locomotives
were employed. Always classified as
a sub-shed of Oswestry, on 19th July
1953, Dean Goods 0-6-0 No 2538 was
recorded outside the shed between
duties.

On leaving Llanidloes, the line progressed into the final river valley it would shadow, that of the Upper Severn. On 13th August 1952, on one of the short workings on the northern part of the line mentioned previously, Dean Goods No 2327 bowls along between Dolwen and Llanidloes with the 12.25pm service from Moat Lane Junction to Llanidloes. The little building to the right of the picture is a platelayers' hut, once a feature seen alongside most railway lines in the country, where the men tasked with looking after the track would keep their tools and have a welcome brew up.

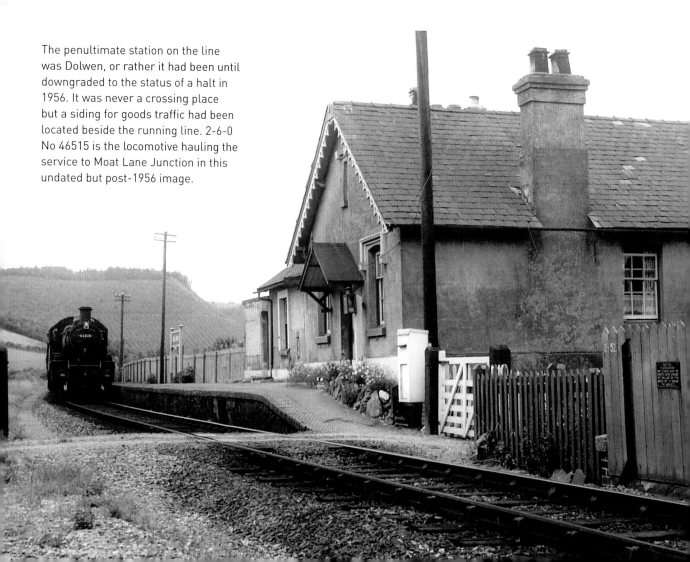

The penultimate station on the line was Dolwen, or rather it had been until downgraded to the status of a halt in 1956. It was never a crossing place but a siding for goods traffic had been located beside the running line. 2-6-0 No 46515 is the locomotive hauling the service to Moat Lane Junction in this undated but post-1956 image.

Llandinam's claim to fame is that it was the birthplace, in 1818, of that great Welsh entrepreneur, David Davies, a one time director of the Cambrian Railways, a mine owner, and the driving force behind the creation of Barry Docks and the railways which served them. The station was a modest affair, with one platform and a few sidings situated on the opposite side of the Severn to the village.

Immediately after leaving Llandinam station, the line crossed the River Severn on this low bridge which had been often damaged by the river over the years, requiring much attention and vigilance from the men of the divisional Bridge Department who were based at Caersws. In the 1950s the third pier from the west bank, seen here, had needed to be replaced. A 2-6-0, No 46401 heads its passenger train across Llandinam Bridge on the last leg of its journey to Moat Lane Junction.

MOAT LANE JUNCTION

On 17th August 1951, ex-GWR Dean Goods class 0-6-0 No 2449 is leaving Moat Lane Junction with a stopping train for Llanidloes. The junction, which was located close to the still open station of Caersws on the line from Shrewsbury to Aberystwyth, took its name from a lane which led to the site of an ancient motte and bailey castle and appeared in the earliest extant timetables, dating from the 1860s. The first trains through here would have been those of the Llanidloes & Newtown Railway, which opened in 1859. It did not become a junction until the arrival of the Newtown & Machynlleth Railway in 1863.

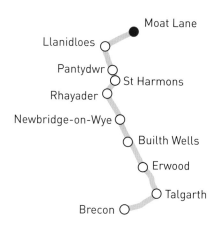

The original railway geography of Moat Lane Junction is clear from this view of Dean Goods No 2449 at the head of the 4.45pm local service to Llanidloes on 9th September 1948. The straight, original alignment of the L&N towards Newtown, which was double-track until 1965, stretches off behind the train. The line to Machynlleth branches off to the left beyond Moat Lane Junction East Signal Box, where the goods train is shunting.

On a murky, damp day in the summer of 1950, conditions not unheard of in this part of Wales, Dean Goods No 2401 brings the stock for a service to Brecon past Moat Lane Junction East Signal Box and towards the platform. The line in the foreground was a run round loop for locomotives on these services.

There are virtually no reminders today that Moat Lane Junction was for a century a large station with four platforms and an important interchange point on the railway network of Mid Wales. The platform on the left was used by the Mid Wales trains and there were three serving the main line, which had at this time trains to Aberystwyth, Pwllheli, Whitchurch and Shrewsbury. In its heyday this busy railway centre also had an engine shed. The station is well filled with trains in this view, taken on 9th August 1948. Coaches for a Mid Wales service sit at their platform to the left, while ex-GWR Dukedog class 4-4-0 No 9026 is blowing off steam impatiently at the head of a stopping train for Whitchurch at one of the main line platforms.

CREDITS

Lost Lines of Wales – The Mid Wales Line
Published in Great Britain in 2017
by Graffeg Limited

Written by Tom Ferris copyright © 2017.
Designed and produced by Graffeg
Limited copyright © 2017

Graffeg Limited, 24 Stradey Park
Business Centre, Mwrwg Road,
Llangennech, Llanelli, Carmarthenshire
SA14 8YP Wales UK Tel 01554 824000
www.graffeg.com

ISBN 9781912050673

1 2 3 4 5 6 7 8 9

Photo credits

© W. A. Camwell/SLS Collection: pages
11, 15, 16, 19, 20, 25, 26, 29, 31, 32, 35, 37,
43, 44, 54, 60, 62, 63.
© R B Parr/Online Transport Archive:
page 12.
© Blake Patterson, Online Transport
Archive: pages 17, 40.
© Kidderminster Railway Museum: pages
21, 23, 36, 38, 39, 41, 46, 47, 48, 51, 52, 55,
56, 59.

Titles in the Lost Lines of Wales series:

Cambrian Coast Line
ISBN 9781909823204

Aberystwyth to Carmarthen
ISBN 9781909823198

Brecon to Newport
ISBN 9781909823181

Ruabon to Barmouth
ISBN 9781909823174

Chester to Holyhead
ISBN 9781912050697

Shrewsbury to Aberystwyth
ISBN 9781912050680

The Mid Wales Line
ISBN 9781912050673

Vale of Neath
ISBN 9781912050666